Original title:
Life's Meaning: Under Construction

Copyright © 2025 Creative Arts Management OÜ
All rights reserved.

Author: Riley Hawthorne
ISBN HARDBACK: 978-1-80566-241-9
ISBN PAPERBACK: 978-1-80566-536-6

## The Story Still in Ink

Once I started writing,
My pen ran out of ink,
A chapter full of blankness,
What did I even think?

Drafts piled high like mountains,
My thoughts just wouldn't land,
A story full of twists,
Yet none of it was planned.

Plot holes like Swiss cheese,
Characters in a swirl,
They dance around the page,
As if in comic twirl.

But every page a treasure,
Each laugh a sweet release,
So here's to all the scribbles,
Our messy minds at peace.

## The Heart's Blueprint

Sketching out my feelings,
With crayons oh so bright,
A blueprint for my heart,
That trails off in mid-flight.

My love's a puzzle piece,
Lost under the couch,
I think I'll go find it,
With a little grunt and crouch.

Each beat a wild rhythm,
Like a cat in a hat,
Who dances on the rooftops,
And never knows what's that.

So let's embrace the chaos,
In this quirky, fun design,
Our hearts are just constructions,
With laughter as the line.

## **Sculpting the Undefined**

With a chisel and a smile,
I carve my dreams in clay,
Each chunk falls to the ground,
Like plans that went astray.

I shape a funny figure,
With arms both wide and short,
A masterpiece of maybes,
In the world's grand art court.

The eyes are bits of laughter,
The nose a silly squint,
This art form keeps evolving,
With every single hint.

So let's mold joy from chaos,
And shape our silly fears,
For sculpting life's oddities,
Can bring us lots of cheers.

## Findings from the Abyss

Down in the depths I wander,
With treasures rare to find,
I gather up my failures,
Each one a little blind.

Lost socks and missing keys,
A goldfish that won't swim,
Are findings from the abyss,
Not quite a fitting whim.

Each stinky little mystery,
Holds laughter in its weight,
So I'll embrace the nonsense,
And celebrate my fate.

In this treasure trove of folly,
I unearth hidden glee,
The absurdity of searching,
Is true fantastic spree!

## The Mosaic of Purpose

Each tile a story, a bit out of place,
Fragments of laughter, some tears to embrace.
Glue them together, with hope and some dots,
Creating a picture of life's tangled plots.

A cat's on a pillow, a dog on the floor,
Building this masterpiece, who could ask for more?
While paint spills and splatters, we dance in the mess,
Constructing our joy in this glorious stress.

## **Tapestry of the Undone**

Woven and tangled, with threads of despair,
A hamster is running; quite frankly, it's rare.
Each stitch holds a secret, a giggle or two,
In this grand old fabric, I'm still finding hue.

With a needle in one hand, some snacks in the other,
Trying to patch up what feels like a clutter.
It's a tapestry wild, full of good-natured jest,
And who said perfection? It's all for the best!

**Navigating the Unfinished**

Maps without compass, I wander the streets,
Trying to learn what perplexes and beats.
A sign says "turn left," but right is so fun,
The journey's the goal, and oh, the rerun!

Lost in my thoughts, stuck in my shoes,
Like tripping on shoelaces, what can you lose?
Collecting adventures, as wild as they come,
Navigating the chaos, oh boy, here we drum!

**Scaffolding of Souls**

Up high on a ladder, I'm painting my dreams,
With brushes of hope, and laughter that beams.
The structure is shaky, but spirits are high,
Building a castle with clouds in the sky.

With each rickety plank, our giggles resound,
Lay down the foundations on shaky ground.
Screw in the joy, and let worries unwind,
Under construction? Nah, we're simply refined!

## Castles in the Solitary Sand

In a world of castles made of grains,
Sand keeps slipping through silly veins.
Builders arrive with their plastic tools,
Claiming kingship, while the ocean drools.

Erecting towers, oh what a feat,
With bucket and spade, a royal seat.
But the tide chuckles, it's a tricky game,
Washing away the prince's acclaim.

Noble knights in flip-flops roam,
Searching for a frosty cone back home.
Yet laughter echoes, sunburns ignite,
As a seagull swoops down for a bite.

In this kingdom of hilarious strife,
We build, we laugh, we skip through life.
With every wave, a lesson to take,
Fleeting dreams in the sandy wake.

## Reflections in Transit

Waiting at the station, it's quite a sight,
With birds on my head, using me for flight.
Trains roll in, then they roll right out,
Confusing my plans without a doubt.

Ticket in pocket, where did it go?
I searched through my bag, but why do I stow?
With coffee in hand, wobbly on my feet,
I realize I'm late—what a silly feat!

Reflections stare back, all tangled hair,
Who's that person with worries to share?
But the mirror just laughs, as I wiggle and sway,
Offers a wink as if to say, "Stay."

As chaos reigns in this travel spree,
I ponder the fuss life throws at me.
Hitching a ride on giggles and dreams,
I find meaning as wild as it seems.

## Horizons Yet to Conquer

Standing on hills with a map distorted,
Eyes on horizons that feel unsupported.
I've plotted the route, but the GPS failed,
And now I'm wading where no one has sailed.

Adventure calls in a high-pitched squeak,
But muddy shoes hide the dreams I seek.
With every step, my whimsy's betrayed,
As I trip over roots like a dance that's replayed.

Climbing the heights, I yell "Ta-da!"
Only to find I'm stuck in a spa.
The view is great but where's the deep thrill?
Chasing sunsets while slipping on a hill.

With snacks in my pocket, I take a big bite,
Laughing at paths that vanish from sight.
Horizons mock with a grin on their face,
But here I am still, lost in my space.

## **Chasing Fractured Dreams**

Once had a dream, oh what a beauty,
But it fractured like glass—such a cutie.
I chased it down paths all crooked and bent,
Bounding with glee where the laughter went.

Running in circles, just like a dog,
Chasing my thoughts through smog and fog.
With every stumble, a chuckle erupts,
As I dive face-first in imaginary cups.

Step back, take stock, what a wild spree,
I capture a wish, but it giggles at me.
It twirls in the air like a kite on a string,
Dodging my grasp, as I dance and sing.

But in fractured dreams, some shine the most,
Where laughter's the key and joy is the host.
So let's gather the shards, make art from the mess,
In every lost chase, there's room for excess.

## Sketches of the Unknown

Woke up today with a plan in my head,
But lost track while dreaming of bread.
Sketches of futures, all out of line,
Yet I giggle at chaos, it's perfectly fine.

Thought I'd be wise, yet I stumbled and fell,
Trip over dreams, but oh, what a swell!
With crayons and markers, I color the day,
Laughing at lines that never obey.

Each step a doodle, a whimsy-filled dance,
Scribbled conclusions, just give them a chance.
In a gallery of giggles, my portrait in view,
The punchline of jokes from my path that I drew.

A canvas of mess, my masterpiece flaws,
Still searching for sense, while life has its laws.
With laughter as paint, I'll splash on the cheer,
Creating a history, one chuckle at a year.

# A Work in Progress

I surveyed my dreams with a frown and a smile,
They all seem to swish, but they're stuck in denial.
Blueprints of hope, they shift like sand,
Guess I'm not ready, just a forecast unplanned.

Brick by brick, I build up my day,
Sometimes it's Lego, sometimes decay.
Under construction, my soul's got flair,
One wall's a window; the other's a chair.

Life in a toolbox, oh, where's my screw?
Searching for answers in the things that I blew.
Tape measure's broken, so wide is my grin,
Patchwork of blunders, that's how I begin.

Each setback a lesson, a laugh or a cheer,
Though my scaffolding wobbles, I've got not a fear.
With humor as hammer, I tackle the mess,
A work in progress, I guess I'm blessed.

## The Forge of Identity

In a workshop of giggles, I hammer and mold,
Chasing sparks of brilliance while sweat trickles cold.
Identity twisted like pretzels in air,
I shape who I am with a comical flair.

Puddles of laughter, I leap in with glee,
Forging my spirit like metal, you see.
The anvil is bouncing, the laughter in tune,
Creating a self that howls at the moon.

Each quirk a feature, each mishap a star,
I'm building my legacy, but where's my car?
With each clang and bang, a character grows,
Silly and strong, like a garden that glows.

So here's to the strange and the wonderfully weird,
In this forge of the self, all doubts disappear.
With merriment bubbling, I stoke the bright fire,
Every laugh's a brick in my growing empire.

## Timelines in Flux

Timeline's a river, it wobbles and bends,
Making up rules while I'm making some friends.
Slipping through moments, oh where will they land?
I'm building a story with a slapstick hand.

Every tick of the clock, a foot in the air,
I trip through the seconds with humorous flair.
Past and future tango, a comical dance,
Fumbling through fate like I'm under a trance.

"Where to now?" I ask with a wink and a nod,
My compass is spinning, the humor's my prod.
In this timeline of giggles, I float like a clown,
Through joys and mishaps, I'm claiming my crown.

Scribbled adventures, like doodles on walls,
Chronicles written in chuckles and brawls.
With fate as a jester, I laugh and I jog,
In the playhouse of time, where I like to hog.

## Journeys in Progress

With each step, I trip and fall,
But laughter echoes, clears the hall.
I gather fragments, bits of cheer,
Each stumble whispers, 'Never fear!'

Maps in hand but lost at sea,
Navigating fun, just me and me.
With socks of stripes and shoes untied,
I dance through doubts, a joyful ride!

Cloudy skies may cloak my way,
But raindrops join the silly play.
With giggles bright and spirits high,
I chase the rainbows in the sky.

So here's to roads that twist and bend,
To laughter shared with every friend.
Let's toast to blunders, big and small,
For in their chaos, we stand tall!

## Visions of the Unseen

I squint and gaze at the blank wall,
Dreams doodled, maybe too small.
With crayons bright, I sketch my fate,
A masterpiece, that's just great!

What if I fly? Or just float?
Perhaps a cow will learn to gloat.
I fish for truths in every sigh,
While pondering why ducks can't fly.

In curious corners of my head,
Ideas bounce like doughnuts spread.
A sprinkling of absurd delight,
Who knew the dark could be so bright?

So here I am, an artist free,
Creating chaos, just to see.
With visions that dance, wiggle, and sway,
I'll laugh and scribble the day away!

## Chisel of Time

With hammer in hand, I tap the stone,
I chip away what's never known.
Each clink is sweet, a funny sound,
As dust clouds form and swirl around.

I sculpt my hopes, my doubts take flight,
With every strike, I find the light.
Though sometimes rough, my edges shine,
Like pizza crust, I'm quite divine!

Patience is key, or so they say,
But then I trip, and what a display!
The sculptor's path is full of laughs,
A comedy of my own gaffes.

So, with each flaw that I embrace,
I carve a smile upon my face.
For every year that's chiseling by,
I learn to laugh, and not just cry!

## The Quest for Essence

In search of treasures, I roam the land,
With mismatched socks and lunch in hand.
Each step, an adventure, wild and bold,
My compass wobbles, but dreams unfold.

I knock on doors with jingling keys,
Some open wide, while others tease.
I ask the stars for hints and signs,
They giggle back in cosmic lines.

I find delight in puzzles strange,
While asking ants if they need change.
The quest gets quirky, full of twist,
Each funny moment, too good to miss.

So here I go, my heart on blast,
In pursuit of essence, not too fast.
With laughter loud, I weave and sway,
A joyful journey, come what may!

## The Journey of a Thousand Sketches

With crayon dreams and paper planes,
We sketch our hopes, dodging the rains.
Drawing futures with vibrant flair,
Smudged cheeky smiles lead us somewhere.

Plans turned doodles, oh what a sight,
We trip on thoughts that take to flight.
A masterpiece or just a joke?
Chasing visions in vibrant smoke.

Each scribble a giggle, each line a jest,
Noses in air, we strut like the best.
To paint our way through laugh and cheer,
Making art from dreams and a cold root beer.

So grab your colors, sketch away fast,
The journey's the fun, and it flies by so fast.
In the gallery of life, we're all quite peculiar,
Creating our canvas in glorious stricture.

# Carpenters of Destiny

With hammers and nails, we build our fate,
Only to find we've forgotten to wait.
Wooden dreams in a workshop mess,
Cutting the corners, hoping for the best.

We measure and ponder, then wing it with flair,
Oops, that board's now a funky chair!
Sawing and laughing as we make our way,
Building strong futures from scraps of the day.

Plumb lines askew, yet we keep on trying,
Sawdust and giggles, no use in crying.
We hammer our hearts into things of delight,
Creating our dreams in the soft candlelight.

As we screw on some laughter, the tweets and the shouts,
We find joy in chaos, in timber, in clouts.
In this workshop of whimsy, we each take our turn,
Crafting our fortunes while candles still burn.

## Illusions of Certainty

I woke up this morning, "What's my plan?"
Grabbed a coffee and hugged my cat Stan.
Intended to conquer the tasks laid ahead,
But tripped on a sock and fell on my bed.

With visions of grandeur, I listed my goals,
But lost my pen while scrolling through scrolls.
Certainty's nice, but I prefer the spins,
Juggling my doubts as the laughter begins.

I signed up for yoga to find my true center,
But ended up in awkward poses—what a mentor!
Each twist and each stretch, a giggle in disguise,
Chasing clarity's shadow while rolling my eyes.

So here's to the chaos, the wobble and whirl,
Embracing the messy, the nitty, the swirl.
In the illusion of wisdom, we swirl round the sun,
Sipping sweet doubts, oh isn't it fun?

**Rays of Uncertain Light**

Beneath the bright glow of the flickering bulb,
We dance in shadows, our worries dissolved.
Who needs a guide in this tangle of night?
We'll just follow the giggles 'til morning's first light.

With lanterns of laughter and torches of cheer,
We stumble on pathways both far and near.
Each step is a game, a stumble, a sprawl,
Searching for wisdom that covers it all.

In the absurdity of wandering trails,
We find our own map while the daylight fails.
Our guiding star's laughter, our compass a grin,
Navigating nonsense, we revel within.

So let's light the way with our quirkiest spark,
As dusk turns to dawn in this whimsical park.
Rays of uncertainty are shining so bright,
Celebrating confusion and laughter tonight!

## Overgrown Pathways of Wonder

In a garden of thoughts, weeds grow tall,
Yet every wild bloom has a tale to call.
With laughter we wander, a map gone astray,
Finding joy in the chaos, come what may.

A squirrel lays claim to my snack for the day,
He chases my dreams in a wild, furry fray.
With each twist and turn on paths we explore,
Who knew life was meant for such comical lore?

The signposts are crooked, the compass is sly,
We'll dance with the wind and giggle at why.
The journey's a riddle, no answers to find,
Yet every odd turn makes us more intertwined.

So let's embrace madness, and whims that ensue,
With friends by our side, we'll make our debut.
In this garden of folly, we'll stake our claim,
For every misstep brings laughter, not shame.

## Chasing the Horizon's Edge

With maps made of dreams and snacks on the side,
We run toward a horizon, where giggles abide.
The sun is our guide, with wild rays that play,
Yet we never quite reach it, but that's okay!

The clouds throw confetti, as jokes fill the air,
A dance of absurdity; we're quite the pair.
With every new challenge, we trip through the breeze,
Bounding back to our feet, with laughter and ease.

The horizon keeps teasing, a wave in its crest,
Yet every missed goal was a funny jest.
With flip-flops as chariots on rough gravel lanes,
We ride through the chaos, ignoring the pains.

For in all of the chasing, we find what we need,
Companionships blooming, we plant every seed.
The edge may elude us, but joy is our pledge,
To savor the journey on this corkscrew hedge.

## Mosaic of Moments

Each moment a tile in this wacky collage,
With giggles and blunders that spark a barrage.
We piece them together with colors so bright,
Crafting a mural of humorous plight.

The cookies that crumble, the soup that's too hot,
We laugh as we savor each culinary plot.
With friends at the table, our hearts intertwine,
In every mishap, we find the divine.

A mosaic of chaos, yet somehow it's whole,
Like socks in the dryer, we search for our soul.
In mismatched adventures, we stumble and trip,
With each quirky twist, we savor the trip.

So here's to the laughter that fills up our days,
To the silly connections that many would praise.
In this artful assembly, we find our own way,
Creating a masterpiece in a humorous fray.

## The Unfinished Tapestry

In a loom where the yarn keeps tangling in knots,
We weave our adventures, with unorthodox dots.
With needles of laughter, we stitch and we sigh,
Creating our fabric while chaos flies by.

The threads may unravel, the colors may clash,
Yet every odd pattern is met with a splash.
As we tumble through moments, unplanned and absurd,
The beauty of messiness sings without words.

Each fray tells a story, each pull has a friend,
As we navigate life, it's not how you mend.
With whims and with wobbles, our tapestry grows,
In stitches of joy, our uniqueness shows.

So let's toast to the threads that we manage to weave,
With humor and heart, there's no need to grieve.
In this unfinished artwork, we find sweet delight,
Living in colors that dance with the light.

## The Colors of Transition

A splash of blue, a dash of red,
My thoughts paint wildly, not a clear thread.
I trip on dreams, laugh in delight,
As colors collide in a joyous flight.

From messy palettes, I craft my way,
With paint-stained hands, I dance and play.
Each shade a giggle, each hue a cheer,
In this grand circus, nothing to fear.

Swirls of orange and splats of green,
My masterpiece grows, though none have seen.
I'll hang it crooked, let it be free,
For who needs standards? Just let it be!

So here's to the chaos, the colors, the fun,
In this vibrant gallery, I'm never done.
With each new brushstroke, I gift a smile,
In this colorful mess, I'll stay awhile.

## **Blueprints of Existence**

I scribble plans on a napkin, see?
A tower of joy, with rooms for tea.
Add some laughter, a sprinkle of play,
Those are the blueprints, come what may!

Engineers frown, they check their stats,
But my plans involve whimsical cats.
A slide from the kitchen, a swing in the hall,
Let's throw in a moat; oh, I'm having a ball!

With duct tape and dreams, I'll build it bright,
A mansion of giggles, through day and night.
"Does that even hold?" they ask in disbelief,
But I wave them away with comedic relief!

So grab your pencils, come sketch along,
In this architect's folly, we can't be wrong!
For in a world full of concrete and fear,
We'll design a kingdom that's ludicrous, dear.

## **Foundations of Tomorrow**

I'm laying bricks made of laughter and fun,
With a shovel of silliness, I'm never done.
Each block is a joke, a giggle, a grin,
A quirky foundation where dreams begin.

The cement? Oh, that's just pizza dough,
Kneaded with humor, watch it grow!
And while the critics may shake their heads,
I'll build a castle where whimsy spreads.

Roofs made of candy, walls of delight,
Every corner contains pure sunshine bright.
No boring blueprints, just a carnival,
In this structure of laughter, we'll stand tall.

So here's to the building, the mess, and the fun,
Creating foundations where quirks weigh a ton.
In the realm of the silly, I'll stake my claim,
For tomorrow is brighter in our giggle game.

## The Canvas of Purpose

On this big canvas, I splash and I throw,
With unexpected colors and strokes that glow.
My purpose is tangled, spinning around,
Yet every odd brushstroke is joyfully found.

I sketch my intentions in blobs and swirls,
With wobbly lines that dance and twirl.
No straight edges allowed, let freedom ring,
In this quirky artwork, I'm everything!

The critics might ponder, "What does it mean?"
But I just chuckle; it's a fun-filled scene!
With splashes of laughter and giggles galore,
Purpose is everywhere if you just explore.

So grab your paint and join in this ride,
Weaving through nonsense, life's painted wide.
With each colorful moment, let joy cohesion,
In this canvas of purpose, embrace our season!

## Bridging Past to Future

In my old shoes, I tripped on memories,
Glimpses of laughter, scattered like leaves.
Building a bridge, plank by plank,
Hoping it holds, while I overthink.

Blueprints scribbled on a napkin late,
With coffee stains marking every fate.
Climbing my ladder towards the unknown,
Could use a map, but I'm lost in my phone.

Constructing dreams with a twist of fate,
Picking up pieces from the wrong crate.
Seems every plan's a jigsaw of jokes,
With each wrong turn, I'm filled with hope.

In this grand project, I'm the foreman too,
With hard hat tilted, and no safety view.
So here's to the chaos, cheers to the fun,
With blueprints confused, let's just run!

Under the sun, I lay my foundation,
Nailing my past with sheer imagination.
Concrete giggles, bricks of surprise,
There's humor in all that we misconceive.

## Navigating the Space In-Between

In the waiting room of what comes next,
I'm juggling dreams like a clown perplexed.
With a popcorn cloud, I float in time,
Snacking on hopes, quite the paradigm.

Maps are for those who know where they're headed,
I'm just here, on a ride that's unthreaded.
Dancing on questions, I'm spinning in place,
With a funhouse mirror, seeing my face.

Between the tick-tock, the moments collide,
I'm surfing on chaos, riding the tide.
With each quirky twist, a new path unfurls,
Like bubble wrap popping in alternate worlds.

Asking the universe for a sign or two,
While it hands me a riddle, just to amuse.
Bubbles of laughter, and giggles galore,
In the space in-between, there's room to explore!

So here's to the in-betweens that we find,
With confusion and laughter, perfectly blind.
Navigating this maze, with love and a grin,
Forever constructing what's waiting within.

## Shadows in the Framework

In a world where blueprints scribble,
Laughter dances, thoughts just giggle.
Nailed together with hopes and schemes,
Shadows flicker as daylight beams.

We hang our wishes on crooked nails,
Jokes float in air like fluttering sails.
The architect chuckles, says it's fine,
As we trip on stories, sip on wine.

Giraffes in hard hats run the show,
While clowns juggle dreams that steal the glow.
The ladder's wobbly; we all just shout,
Constructing joy without a doubt.

So here we build with laughter loud,
A quirky house, our goofy crowd.
With echoes of joy filling each room,
We paint our lives with vibrant bloom.

## The Architect of Dreams

Sketches scribbled on napkin seams,
Waltz with whimsy, play with dreams.
Blueprints fly like paper planes,
While chaos dances in quirky chains.

Chasing purpose like a wild hare,
With plans that never quite prepare.
Swirling paint and mismatched bricks,
Here we giggle, pulling crazy tricks.

Drafting wishes on a foggy night,
Fumbling plans, yet feeling light.
The architect struggles with a grin,
"Who needs a map when joy's within?"

Laughter's the cement, humor the steel,
Constructing futures that brightly feel.
With playful heart, we bend the rules,
In the land of dreams, we are all fools.

## Scaffolding the Soul

Balancing hopes on rickety beams,
Dancing on clouds while sipping creams.
Laughter echoes in every bend,
As we scaffold joy, our happy friend.

Big ideas bubble like fizzy drinks,
With every mix, the world winks.
Our souls stretch in ridiculous ways,
Painting our truths in silly displays.

The tower sways, but we won't fall,
For humor's the net that catches all.
In the chaos of our wild delight,
We build our own stars, shining bright.

So hand me a wrench and I'll brew a joke,
Together we laugh as our plans provoke.
With each new layer, we toast and sing,
Our souls scaffolded in everything.

## Laying Stones of Purpose

Each stone we lay, a giggle found,
In silly shapes, like wacky mounds.
Purpose rolls like a bouncing ball,
As we stack our hopes, we hear the call.

With wiggly worms as our guide,
We joke about the aimless ride.
Purpose slips, then doubles back,
On this road of whimsy, we lose the track.

Bricks are whispers, laughter loud,
Building castles in the fluffy cloud.
Rummaging treasures through piles of fun,
Each stone a story, connecting one.

So, toss a stone, see where it lands,
Destiny dances with playful hands.
Laying down dreams, no need to roam,
In our goofy hearts, we find a home.

## **Bridges of Experience**

We build our bridges, one plank at a time,
With laughter and glue, oh isn't it sublime?
Crossing the gaps, we stumble and sway,
"Hold on tight!" we yell, as we drift away.

A friend trips and falls, into puddles galore,
'Just testing the load!' he laughs as he swore,
With each little mishap, we learn and we grow,
Our bridges get stronger, with every woe.

We navigate trolls, and a goat or two,
'Is that bridge to nowhere? It sure looks askew!'
But we carry on laughing, with hearts full of cheer,
Each misstep a story, that brings us more near.

So here's to the bridges, both rickety and tough,
To the memories made, and the moments we bluff,
It's a wild construction, with friends by your side,
Building our futures, with joy and with pride.

## Whispers of the Infinite

In a cosmos so vast, we're but squeaks in the void,
Finding meaning in chaos, often unalloyed.
With wishes like confetti, we toss into space,
Hoping to catch them, a cosmic embrace.

A star winks and giggles, 'What's the fuss down there?'
'We're busy creating!' We shout with a flare.
But the planets just spin and the comets, they hum,
'Just keep on your quest, you silly ol' chum.'

Existence a riddle, a puzzle to tease,
We dance with absurdity, looking for keys.
While time plays its tricks, like a jester in tow,
We stumble through whispers, as we ebb and we flow.

So raise up your glasses, to wonders unseen,
To the jokes of the universe, funny and keen,
For in all of the chaos, we find what we seek,
The giggle of existence, so bright and unique.

## The Craft of Tomorrow

With tools made of dreams, we sculpt and we mold,
Creating tomorrow from stories retold.
Each laugh is a chisel, each giggle a brush,
Crafting our futures in a colorful rush.

We hammer out hopes, while tripping on fears,
Mixing joy with our doubts, and shedding some tears.
A swing of our mallet sends worries away,
Building tomorrows, come join in the play!

With sketches on napkins, our visions take flight,
We craft with abandon, from morning till night.
While some may just fumble, oh others will soar,
The craft of tomorrow is never a bore.

So gather your pals, let's craft what we can,
With laughter our glue, united we stand,
The masterpiece's waiting, let's throw on some flair,
Tomorrow's a canvas, a chance to declare.

## Paths Yet Traced

We wander the pathways, not knowing the bends,
With maps drawn in crayon and laughter, our friends.
Each step is a riddle, each corner a jest,
Finding joy in the journeys, not quests for the best.

With shoes that are squeaky and hats on our heads,
We giggle through forests and hop over beds.
A squirrel gives directions, with nods and some flair,
As we trot through the bushes, we skip and we dare.

The trails are a puzzle, a maze with no choice,
Yet we keep moving forward, with each silly voice.
With chiming of laughter, we push through the haze,
The paths that we wander, are sunshine and rays.

So here's to our journeys, uncharted and fun,
With each twist and turn, our hearts come undone.
For at the end of our path, another will greet,
Another adventure, a new song to beat.

## Blueprints of Existence

I drew my plans with crayons bright,
Each squiggle was a new delight.
A staircase leads to nowhere high,
I wonder if it's time to fly.

My architect is just a cat,
She knocks my dreams down with a pat.
Every model's just a laugh,
Who knew a pie chart could be half?

The windows look out on a wall,
The door won't open, what a stall!
Yet still I chase that fun-filled spark,
If only I could find the park.

So here I stand with blueprints wide,
Hoping for a joyful ride.
Mistakes become a houses' charm,
With laughter loud, it's safe from harm.

## Foundations of Thought

I built my base on jelly beans,
With marshmallow walls, or so it seems.
Thoughts bounce around like ping pong balls,
Each idea either soars or falls.

Foundations wobbly, but oh so sweet,
I dance atop, I tap my feet.
Wobbling thoughts from yesterday,
Still make me grin in a silly way.

Construction hats are on quite tight,
As I navigate through day and night.
With a sledgehammer made of cheese,
I laugh out loud and feel at ease.

So here's to thoughts, building anew,
With laughter as the perfect glue.
And when it shakes, I'll wear a smile,
Imperfect, but it's worth the while.

**Echoes of Tomorrow**

I shouted at the world today,
And it echoed back, 'Just play!'
Tomorrow's plans are in a jam,
With peanut butter, oh, how glam!

The future's bright, like neon lights,
Painted dreams in silly sights.
I'll ride my dreams like roller coasters,
With ups and downs, and giggly roasters.

Tomorrow giggles just like me,
A dance of options, wild and free.
So let's hop on this funny train,
Where joy's the ticket and love's the gain.

Echoes play a cheerful tune,
Under the laugh of the sun and moon.
Join the chorus, sing along,
Life's mischief is where we belong.

## Fragments of a Journey

I packed my bags with odd-shaped socks,
A road map drawn with silly doodles and locks.
Fragments of path and silly signs,
Which way to go? There are no lines!

The signs all read, 'Take the wrong way!'
With laughter ringing, come what may.
Adventure calls in a quirky text,
Where whimsy waits—what comes next?

I stumbled on a rainbow trail,
Met a talking fish who told a tale.
Each twist and turn a comic scene,
Journey's odd, but it's the in-between!

So here I go on paths unknown,
With jester's cap and a heart of stone.
Fragments of joy by starlight's glow,
Won't you join me? Let's steal the show.

## **Echoes in the Framework**

Woke up today with plans in mind,
Only to find the coffee's blind.
The cat's on the keyboard, typing a note,
Saying, 'This is chaos, not a boat!'

Found the hammer, but it went missing,
Nailed my thumb and started hissing.
Blueprints scattered, like leaves in fall,
Guess I'll just build my dream out of squall.

Every corner's got a funny twist,
I'm a carpenter, not a sculptor, missed.
Laughter echoes in the empty room,
With a tape measure that goes whoosh and zoom.

Yet in this mess, I yeah, I find,
That the fun of creating is never blind.
So pass me the glue, let's stick it right,
And dance with the chaos, what a sight!

## Unraveled Threads of Being

I bought some yarn to knit a dream,
But tangled up, it's a comedy theme.
My needles broke, my patterns too,
Yet here I sit, with socks for a zoo.

Called for help but got a clown,
With polka dots and a floppy gown.
Together we laughed at the bits we spun,
Turned chaos to joy, oh what fun!

Unraveled threads scattered about,
Like thoughts of wonder dancing about.
Each knot a riddle, each weave a laugh,
Pick up the pieces, or just take a nap.

In the fabric of this wacky piece,
I find my bliss and a burst of peace.
So stitch away, my clumsy friend,
This wobbly journey will never end!

## Dreams in the Making

Building castles out of sand and dreams,
With marshmallow towers bursting at the seams.
A seagull swoops down for a tasty bite,
And I'm left laughing, what a silly sight!

My friend's a painter with colors so bright,
But spills orange juice, oh what a fright!
Her canvas turns into a splashy mess,
And still we giggle at our boldness, yes!

Our dreams take shape, like fluffy clouds,
Each one different, none the same, proud.
Yet when the rain comes, we don't run away,
We grab our umbrellas and join in the play.

In this playful art, we find our way,
Constructing joy at the end of the day.
So let's raise a brush to the fun we make,
In this whimsical world, no hearts can break!

## Fragments of a Future

I found a map to nowhere, oh dear,
X marks the spot for a picnic here!
With ants as my crew, we feast in the sun,
Sipping lemonade, oh this is fun!

Pieces of dreams scattered like stars,
These glittering wishes can't be too far.
A paper airplane flies with glee,
Chasing the future, just wait and see!

A broken clock tells tales of time,
Every tick a joke, every tock a rhyme.
While waiting for fate, I munch on a snack,
Who knew building hopes could be a laugh track?

So here's to the puzzles of days gone by,
Constructing a future that's a sweet pie.
With laughter and friends, we'll find our way,
In this whimsical dance, come what may!

## Beneath the Surface

Under the clouds, plans in disarray,
A wobbly ladder, I climbed today.
With hammers and nails, I try to create,
A house full of joy, no room for fate.

Noodles in broth, a masterpiece dire,
Trying to cook while my dreams catch fire.
With socks that don't match, life's quite a spree,
A circus unfolds, come laugh with me!

Jigsaw of laughter in pieces so bright,
A puzzle of quirks, my morning delight.
Wearing a cape, I'm a superhero,
But tripping on shoelaces is what steals the show.

Beneath the surface, chaos is fun,
Twirling in circles, I'm never the one.
With smiles unpolished, we dance in the rain,
Life's a grand jigsaw, let's slip on the train.

## Anticipating the Unwritten

Plans crumpled like paper, optimism's foe,
I scribble my dreams, then out they all go.
A map with no markers, just arrows that twist,
Anticipating stories that can't be dismissed.

The clock's losing tick-tock makes time seem a joke,
While coffee spills over on all of my notes.
Tickling the future with whimsical cheer,
Who knows what's ahead, or just lurking near?

Muffin crumbs scatter, a breakfast debate,
Jelly on toast, oh, what a fate!
Anticipating laughter and goofy pursuits,
Chasing a squirrel while looking for roots.

Mind like a rollercoaster, twists, and turns,
Writing my script as the whole page burns.
With chuckles and doodles, I dance through the fray,
Anticipating surprises that come out to play.

## The Construct of Self

Brick by brick, I build my persona,
With googly eyes, my emotional zona.
Glued pieces of laughter, humor's my tool,
The construct of self is both silly and cool.

Wrenches and pencils, my toolbox in hand,
Screws of uncertainty help me to stand.
Wobbly walls, yet my spirit's alive,
I'm crafting a version of me that can thrive.

With paint that drips down from a brush out of hand,
A masterpiece grows, though not as I planned.
Failures like glitter stick to my shoes,
They sparkle and shine, it's okay to lose!

At times I'm a castle, at times just a shed,
Building a kingdom of thoughts in my head.
In this funny construction, I take a grand fall,
But laughter's the glue that holds up it all.

## Time's Fragile Fabric

Threads that unravel, oh look at that mess,
I'm stitching my stories with thoughts of finesse.
Needles of hope, they poke and they prod,
Time's fragile fabric, odd patterns applaud.

Woven in laughter, the past takes a bow,
"Where's the instruction manual?" I ask and wow!
Dancing with minutes that slip through my hands,
While socks disappear, defying all plans.

Tangled in stories, I laugh as I weave,
Crafting my narrative, who would believe?
Each patch a memory, ridiculous thread,
While time's gentle whispers dance round in my head.

So here's to the fabric we stitch on our way,
Designing a quilt made of joyful dismay.
With colors so wild and patterns so bright,
Time's funny design makes everything right.

## Renovating the Heart

In the workshop where I spend my days,
I hammer thoughts like crooked nails.
With bright ideas and silly plans,
I paint my dreams in colorful swirls.

Each room needs laughter, a little decor,
Some puns plastered on the wall.
Every patch of joy is a work in progress,
As I stumble through the light-hearted brawl.

I find lost socks in the corners galore,
They serve as my quirky muse.
In my heart, there's always a draft,
Bursting with fun, never to lose.

I'm remodeling with glee, it's a jolly affair,
Laughter echoes in every frame.
The blueprint's a mess, but who really cares?
It's a joyful disaster, and that's my game.

## The Canvas of Experience

I brush my days with colors bold,
Splashes of chaos dance like clowns.
My palette's messy, a joyful scene,
Where even sadness wears a crown.

Each stroke's a story, a laugh, a tear,
I daub the sky with polka dots.
In the gallery of moments, I twist and turn,
Creating shapes that tie up knots.

Framed by the absurd in every hue,
Uncertainty adds a funny twist.
I stand before this jigsawed art,
And giggle at the things I've missed.

A canvas wet with dreams unplanned,
Crisis mingles with pure delight.
In the showcase of experience, I grin wide,
For every blunder turns to light.

## Threads of Uncertainty

I knit my hopes with mismatched yarns,
A tangled web of dreams and fears.
With every stitch, I crack a smile,
Turning worries into gentle cheers.

Knots and loops in patterns strange,
Life's a scarf that sways askew.
I'll wear it proudly, odd and bright,
Each thread tells tales that are quite askew.

Sometimes a frog hops in my lap,
Of troubles learned from folly's jest.
I unravel problems with a chuckle,
Finding humor in what's detest.

As colors blend in unexpected ways,
My strange design is truly free.
In this sweater of haphazard grace,
I find the joy in a tangled spree.

## The Dawn of Discovery

Today I woke with a silly thought,
That wanderlust is quite profound.
I'll uncover mysteries in my backyard,
A treasure map just waiting to be found.

I'll chase the squirrels, follow the ants,
With a magnifying glass in hand.
Every leaf's an ancient scroll,
A laugh-filled journey, oh so grand!

With each new dawn, I trip and fumble,
I trip over wisdom in the grass.
The world is vast, yet close at heart,
I giggle at the moments that pass.

Unraveling surprises wrapped in light,
Each day's a ride, a whimsical fest.
The dawn brings wonders, silly delights,
In this discovery, I find my quest.

## The Symphony of Uncertainty

In a world of baffling charms,
I searched for notes amidst alarms.
My plans like jelly on a plate,
Wobble and dance, oh isn't fate!

With every step, I trip and sway,
The map I drew has gone astray.
But in this comic, grand parade,
I find the joy that won't degrade.

I juggle dreams and tangled threads,
A circus act in daily spreads.
Is there a rhythm to this tune?
Maybe ninjas dance with the moon!

So grab a laugh, don't take a squeeze,
Embrace the chaos, swing with ease.
Let awkward moments take the stage,
A life well-rehearsed is dull and sage!

## Constructs of the Heart

I built a castle made of smiles,
With rooms for all my quirky trials.
But bricks of laughter came undone,
And left me standing in the sun!

Blueprints drawn on crumpled napkins,
Sketching hopes and hasty wrinklins.
"Oh look!" I shout, "a wall of glee!"
Turns out it's just a part of me.

Each room's a choice, a whimsy feat,
With mismatched chairs and funky heat.
A dance floor made of peanut shells,
Where every mishap sweetly dwells.

So let's embrace these slapstick ways,
Constructing love in wild arrays.
In every flaw, a chuckle starts,
A story framed in silly parts!

## Notes from a Draft

My life is scribbles on a page,
A messy plot, a wooden stage.
Characters that swap and prance,
In scenes where nothing goes as planned.

Each chapter starts with grand intent,
Then veers off like a wayward tent.
With punchlines lurking near the prose,
I find the joy in all that blows.

Plot twists come in shades of doubt,
Yet laughter's what it's all about.
A first draft's chaos feels just right,
As I pen down this comedic flight.

So here I scribble, scratch, and scrawl,
A story woven through it all.
With every mess, there's something neat,
A party where the blunders meet!

## Threads of Intent

I weave my thoughts with yarn and thread,
A tapestry of smiles ahead.
With every stitch a whimsy scene,
An artwork made of hopes unseen.

I unravel yarns of dreams not tied,
And knit a quilt that's full of pride.
"Oops!" I gasp, as colors clash,
Yet in this mess, my heart will splash.

Each tangled knot becomes a tale,
Of daring leaps and epic fails.
With fabric snips and laughter shared,
I make a blanket, fully bared.

So let's embrace this patchwork spree,
A quilt of joy for you and me.
In every thread, a chuckle laced,
A cozy world, our lives embraced!

## **Building Bridges to Self**

I tried to build a bridge today,
But forgot to check the map,
I ended up quite far away,
Stuck inside a friendly gap.

With planks of dreams and nails of hope,
I thought I'd sail, but took a dip,
I found out bridges need some rope,
And maybe a more steady grip.

I laughed aloud at my mistake,
As ducks began to quack and tease,
Turns out this bridge is just a fake,
It leads straight to a patch of cheese!

So here I sit and munch away,
Building bridges made of brie,
With every bite, I'd like to say,
I'm still constructing me!

## Crumbling Walls and New Paths

The walls I built, they start to crack,
Each brick of doubt falls down with ease,
I thought I'd fear the big setback,
But turns out it's a gentle breeze.

Now with a smile, I watch them fall,
Like autumn leaves in swirling dance,
I wave goodbye; they had a ball,
And now I've got a fresh romance.

New paths appear like magic tricks,
As clowns invade my dreary space,
They juggle dreams and silly flicks,
And leave me with a clownish face!

So let's toast to the walls we broke,
And pour some juice inside a hat,
For every stumble is a joke,
And laughter is where we're at!

## The Symphony of Beginnings

A trumpet plays a clumsy tune,
While violins are lost in time,
But all together, night or noon,
We dance to each off-beat chime.

The flutes are busy with a snack,
While cellos string a silly tale,
In harmony, they all just hack,
Yet somehow, still, we shall not fail.

Who knew beginnings could be fun?
With all this noise, it's quite absurd,
A symphony of goofy run,
Each note a laugh, a joyous word!

So join the team, put on your hat,
And play your part with style and cheer,
For life's a concert, imagine that,
A playful tune, forever near!

## Underneath the Surface

They say the truth hides down below,
Like gophers in a sunlit park,
But what I found was quite a show,
A dance of quirks, all bright and stark.

Each secret just a silly prank,
Like clowns that trip on jelly beans,
Unpacking thoughts from shadowed tanks,
Reveals the laughter in our scenes.

Underneath, a party's near,
Where jokes and dreams collide like play,
With every giggle, drop a tear,
And swim in joy, come what may!

So here's to depths where oddities blend,
Embrace the quirks, let worries cease,
For under all, we just pretend,
That life's a jolly piece of cheese!

# Playgrounds of Possibility

In the sandbox of dreams, we all play,
Building castles that wash away.
Swinging high while the clouds bury,
Just waiting for gravity to be a little less scary.

Slides that twist, and merry-go-rounds,
In this game of life, who's keeping the bounds?
Laughing with friends, we stumble and trip,
With scraped-up knees, we still make our grip.

Seesaws rise with a bounce and a thud,
Every fall's just a splash in the mud.
Chasing butterflies, we trip on our shoes,
In playgrounds of dreams, we're always amused.

Though life might seem like a chaotic spree,
In the sandpit of laughter, we're wild and free.
So we kick off our shoes and willfully roam,
In the land of make-believe, we're finally home.

## Dust and Enlightenment

Amid the chaos, a speck of dust,
Rides a beam of light with nary a fuss.
Floating high in a world of dread,
It whispers, 'Relax, and just go ahead!'

Life's a construction site where hammers slam,
With sparks flying like glitter in jam.
Just clear the sawdust and take a peek,
The path to wisdom isn't always sleek.

In the attic of thoughts, we stumble and trip,
Finding treasures wrapped in bubble wrap dip.
Laughter echoes in this dusty old space,
Where enlightenment wears a funny old face.

So, grab a broom, sweep the cobwebs away,
Let's dance with the dust; it's a sweep-up ballet.
With each little laugh, there's a nugget to gain,
In the mess of our minds, we've got nothin' to feign.

## **Reflections in a Broken Mirror**

In shards of glass, I see my grin,
A patchwork of me, where do I begin?
Each crack tells a story of lessons learned,
The funny side of life is surely earned.

Reflections warped and wobbly too,
In this circus of self, who's fooling who?
Juggling doubts in a three-ring show,
With every stumble, just more room to grow.

Funny how thoughts can twist and shout,
In a broken mirror, the truth's all about.
Embrace the chaos, wear it with flair,
For in every misstep, there's joy to share.

So gather the pieces; let's build a new way,
With laughter as glue, we'll brighten the day.
In this carnival of what's real and not,
A cracked-up reflection is all we've got.

## The Puzzle of Being

A thousand pieces scattered around,
Finding corners on this merry-go-round.
With a cat in hand and a dog by my side,
We laugh at the chaos; there's nowhere to hide.

The picture is muddled; oh, what a sight!
Yet here in the mess, we're filled with delight.
Try fitting a square in a round little hole,
With each laugh echoing, we feel more whole.

Puzzling together without missing a beat,
Trading wrong edges for something so sweet.
In this game of assembly, we forget all the woes,
Piecing together a life built on prose.

So here's to the jigsaw, the quirky and fun,
With laughter our compass, we're never outrun.
In the wild art of being, we'll cherish the thrill,
For each piece that fits brings us closer still.

## Fractals of Existence

In knots and loops we spin around,
A dance of chaos, sound and sound.
Each step we take, a twist of fate,
In this wild world, we navigate.

Like pizza slices cut too thin,
We search for meaning, a sliver within.
Laughter echoes through the maze,
A jester's grin in silly ways.

## **Vessels of Exploration**

With a hat on the head and map in hand,
We're off to seek the puzzling land.
A ship made of dreams, it might just sink,
But we'll laugh so hard, we won't even think.

Navigating storms with ice cream cones,
The ocean of life with all its tones.
We'll find new worlds or just lost keys,
In our quirky boat that creaks and wheezes.

## The Palette of Possibility

With paintbrush in hand and colors to mix,
We splash our hopes and a few funny tricks.
The canvas awaits, what will we choose?
A world of wonders, a riotous muse.

Splattered dreams in vibrant hues,
Maybe we'll make a masterpiece, or two.
Or perhaps just a smudge, a giggle or two,
A canvas, a mess, oh what shall we do?

## **Pages Yet to be Turned**

Books stacked high, tales yet untold,
Turning the pages, we're feeling bold.
Characters dancing, some trip and fall,
In our funny story, there's room for all.

With every chapter, a wink and a nudge,
A plot twist coming, oh what a grudge!
Life's a novel, with scribbles and cheer,
Let's pen our laughter, leave out the fear.

## Sketches of Significance

With crayons in hand, I start to draw,
A masterpiece flawed, full of awe.
The lines are wobbly, the colors clash,
But every mistake's just part of the splash.

A house made of jelly, a fence made of cheese,
A dog that can talk, oh please!
The laughter erupts, it's quite the scene,
In this gallery of quirky routine.

## The Art of Becoming

I'm painting my future, with paintbrush in hand,
But sometimes I spill, then I just stand.
Do I clean it up, or let it be art?
Perhaps it's expressive, a brand new start!

My reflection giggles, it's quite a sight,
With mismatched socks and hair that's a fright.
I toast to the chaos, a bold operation,
Here's to the journey of self-creation!

## Footprints in the Dust

Stumbling through moments, I trip on my shoes,
Leave footprints of laughter, forgetful hues.
"Where are we going?" says my pet rock,
To the land of misfits? Oh, what a shock!

The road is a puzzle, with pieces askew,
Like socks in the dryer, what's old is now new.
I'll dance through the mess, with joy on my face,
In a world full of whimsy, I'm finding my place.

## Embers of Potential

With a spark in my heart, I light the night,
I'm cooking up dreams that take flight.
The smoke is a tickle, it makes me sneeze,
But oh, the flavors, they aim to please!

I stir a few wishes, I bake some delight,
Hoping the oven won't take a bite.
It's messy and silly, this recipe true,
But it's all made with laughter; so, cheers to the brew!

# Foundations of the Unsung

In a world of blueprints drawn,
We trip on echoes of the dawn.
With coffee spills and wobbly chairs,
We build our dreams without any cares.

The jackhammers sing a rhythmic tune,
As we dance beneath the lazy moon.
Our plans might wobble, our walls might bend,
But what's construction without a friend?

We mix our joy in cemented cracks,
Laughter lingers, never looks back.
Blue skies above, we hope, we scheme,
We're all just actors in a funny dream.

So grab your hard hats and start to shout,
The work is messy, that's what it's about.
We lay the bricks, we crack some jokes,
In this silly world, we are the folks.

## The Frame of Tomorrow

Nailing beams, a splash of paint,
Our plans are wild, they hardly faint.
Constructing futures, we stumble and trip,
With pizza slices and a soda sip.

The architect says, 'What's this design?'
We laugh so hard, it feels divine.
With crooked angles and a plumb line,
We toast to structures yet to shine.

As we weld our hopes with a gentle spark,
We chase the dreams that light the dark.
Tomorrow beckons, we can't resist,
But first, let's add a metal twist!

So here's to frames that twist and sway,
Who knew the blueprints led astray?
With humor and heart, we'll break the mold,
In this grand tale, our laughter's bold!

## **Lines in the Sand**

With a bucket and spade, we start our play,
Building castles that wash away.
Here comes the tide, let's quickly flee,
Our dreams are sandy, but we're so free!

We draw our plans with careless glee,
Then laugh as waves claim our decree.
'This won't hold,' we all declare,
Yet every grain brings joy to share.

The gulls above caw giant laughs,
As we craft our destiny from silly drafts.
Forget the bricks, let's just pretend,
With whims and wishes, we'll never end!

Waves roll in, our structures fall,
But here we stand, we're having a ball.
In dreams of sand, we live, we play,
With twinkling eyes, we seize the day!

## The Colors of Incompletion

With paintbrushes dancing, we splatter cheer,
The vision's a mess, but we hold it dear.
A splash of purple, a touch of green,
Our canvas is wild, undefined, unseen.

To finish a mural would be too tame,
We giggle and plot in a colorful game.
Where orange meets blue in a wonderful clash,
We're painting our world in a vibrant splash.

The strokes are bold, the lines a bit hazy,
We find our joy in chaos so crazy.
'What's a deadline?' we cheerfully muse,
With our heartbeats loud, we cannot lose!

So here's to colors that never set straight,
In this unfinished art, we celebrate fate.
We'll swirl our hearts on this vibrant stage,
In the masterpiece of the amusing age!

## **Rebuilding the Invisible**

I found a blueprint made of dreams,
With colors bright and silly schemes.
I tripped on beams and laughed so loud,
Mistakes were gold—oh, how they proud!

The hard hat was a gift from fate,
It fits my head, but not so straight.
Building castles out of foam,
Who knew my tools could call this home?

Ladders leaning, yet I climb,
Singing songs of jumbled rhyme.
The blueprints danced just out of reach,
As joy became my only speech.

So here I craft with playful flair,
Constructing dreams from thin air.
With every giggle, every plight,
The invisible shines in the light.

## **An Odyssey of Today**

I set sail on a cardboard boat,
With rubber ducks, we drift and float.
The winds of chaos blow so strong,
Yet even storms can't feel so wrong.

Maps are scribbles on the floor,
Each X marks laughter, maybe more.
Today's adventure starts with spice,
Guessing if I'll roll the dice.

Pirate dreams of Swedish meatballs,
Yo-ho-ho in grocery halls.
With every giggle, we dare to roam,
In aisles of wonder, we find our home.

No treasure chests but snacks galore,
In this story, who needs folklore?
An odyssey of misfit cheer,
Navigating moments, oh my dear!

## Shadows of the Aspirant

I'm casting shadows, drawing lines,
With big dreams wrapped in silly signs.
An aspiring star on wobbling feet,
My shadow dances to its own beat.

I scribble plans on a napkin square,
With hopes that float like fluffy air.
But every step feels slightly off,
Just one more trip—oh, what a scoff!

With coffee cups as safety nets,
My shadow laughs, no regrets.
We juggle plans and coffee mugs,
Unruly dreams and playful hugs.

Oh, the art of not being meek,
Painting futures with every squeak.
Through trials great and giggles bold,
In shadows' light, our dreams unfold.

## The Architecture of Hope

I built a tower made of dreams,
With popsicle sticks and laughter beams.
It swayed a bit, oh what a sight,
But hope's a song that feels so right.

Blueprints folded in my hat,
Plans so wild, they look like chat.
With every sketch that goes awry,
They float like kites that learn to fly.

In this structure made of cheer,
I find my purpose growing near.
With each new block, I guffaw,
Creating patterns that make me awe.

So come and join this messy quest,
With laughter loud, we build our best.
In the architecture of our play,
Hope stands tall—come what may!

## Mending the Invisible

Thread by thread, we stitch with care,
A quilt of dreams, but not a square.
Each patch a tale, quirky and bright,
With mismatched socks, it's quite a sight.

We sew a smile, we patch a laugh,
In life's fabric, we find our path.
Though seams may fray and colors clash,
Our crafty hearts ignite a splash.

In this quirky work, we learn to cope,
With safety pins and a bit of hope.
A snip here, a tuck there, a goofy grin,
We mend the holes that life's put in.

So grab your needles and let's create,
A tapestry weird, but isn't it great?
For in each stitch, there's joy and jest,
In our fabric fun, we're truly blessed.

## Unveiling the Hidden

Behind every door that squeaks and creaks,
Lurk oddball finds and silly sneaks.
A sock that's lost, half a puzzle piece,
An ancient card in a thickening crease.

We dig through boxes filled with dust,
In search of treasures, it's a must.
But all we find are sticky notes,
With doodled cats in tiny boats!

The hidden gems of yesterday,
Hold quirky secrets in their sway.
A floppy disk? What's that for now?
It makes us ponder, we scratch our brow.

Yet through the chaos, laughter flows,
As we uncover what no one knows.
With each odd find, we raise a cheer,
In our treasure hunt, we find good cheer.

## Threads of the Unsung

From tangled yarn to unspooled string,
We weave a tale that has no king.
Each knot and twist, a nonsensical plan,
The art of crafting smiles, oh man!

The thread goes wild, it dances free,
Like thoughts gone haywire, just like me.
A paperclip here, a crayon there,
We stitch our fables without a care.

The unsung threads in a vibrant weave,
Hold stories spun, we all believe.
With hands a-fumbling, joy we glean,
In this wild craft, we're all routine.

So gather round, let's make a scene,
With laughter's thread, we'll intervene.
For in this chaos, we find our song,
With jumbled stitches where we belong.

## Fleeting Moments in Design

Kaleidoscopes of glitters and glue,
Fleeting moments, a magical view.
A doodle here, a splash of paint,
In this mad world, who's a saint?

With rulers bent and ideas askew,
We sketch our day, a hodgepodge crew.
But who needs straight lines, let's be bold,
In crooked drawings, adventures unfold.

Chairs that wobble, tables that sway,
Designs that dance in an absurd play.
We laugh at blooms that never seem real,
Creating chaos is part of the deal.

So throw on a hat that's oversized,
In quirky attire, we shall rise.
For in fleeting moments of whimsical cheer,
We find the joy... and hold it dear.

www.ingramcontent.com/pod-product-compliance
Lightning Source LLC
Chambersburg PA
CBHW071848160426
43209CB00003B/470